I0163543

TAWDRY
Have you put a Bill on your Door, Ma'am, as you said you would?

HAYCOCK
It is up, it is up. Oh Tawdry! that a Woman who hath been bred, and always lived like a Gentlewoman, and followed a polite way of Business, should be reduced to let Lodgings.

TAWDRY
It is a melancholy Consideration truly.

[Knocking.

But hark! I hear a Coach stop.

HAYCOCK
Some Rake or other, who is too poor to have any Reputation. This is not a Time of Day for good Customers to walk abroad. The Citizens, good Men! can't leave their Shops so soon.

[**SERVANT** enters.

SERVANT
Madam, a Gentleman and Lady to enquire for Lodgings; they seem to be just come out of the Country, for the Coach and Horses are in a terrible dirty Pickle.

HAYCOCK
Why don't you shew them in? Tawdry, who knows what Fortune hath sent us?

TAWDRY
If she had meant me any Good, she'd have sent a Gentleman without a Lady.

[**SERVANT** returning with **JOHN**.

SERVANT
This is my Mistress, Friend.

JOHN
Do you take Volks in to live here? Because if you do, Madam and the Squire will come and live with you.

HAYCOCK
Then your Master is a Squire, Friend, is he?

JOHN
Ay, he is as good a Squire as any within five Miles o' en: Tho'f he was but a Footman before, what is that to the purpose? Madam has enough for both o' 'em.

HAYCOCK

Well, you may desire your Master and his Lady to walk in. I believe I can furnish them with what they want. What think you, Tawdry, of the Squire and his Lady, by this Specimen of them?

TAWDRY
Why I think if I can turn the Squire to as good Account as you will his Lady, (I mean if she be handsome,) we shall have no reason to repent our Acquaintance. You will soon teach her more Grace, than to be pleased with a Footman, especially as he is her Husband.

HAYCOCK
Truly, I must say, I love to see Ladies prefer themselves. Mercy on those who betray Women to sacrifice their own Interest: I would not have such a Sin lie on my Conscience for the World.

[Enter **MR. THOMAS**, **WIFE**, and **SERVANTS**.

MR. THOMAS
Madam, your humble Servant. My Fellow here tells me you have Lodgings to lett, pray what are they, Madam?

HAYCOCK
Sir, my Bill hath informed you.

MR. THOMAS
Pox! I am afraid she suspects I can't read.

HAYCOCK
What Conveniencies, Madam, would your Ladyship want?

WIFE
Why, good Woman, I shall want every thing which other fine Ladyships want. Indeed, I don't know what I shall want yet; for I never was in Town before: But I shall want every thing I see.

MR. THOMAS
I hope your Apartments here are handsome, and that People of Fashion use to lodge with you.

HAYCOCK
If you please, Sir, I'll wait on your Honour, and shew you the Rooms.

MR. THOMAS
Ay do, do so; do wait on me. John, do you hear, do you take care of all our Things.

WIFE
Ay pray, John, take care of the great Cake and the cold Turkey, and the Ham and the Chickens, and the Bottle of Sack and the two Bottles of Strong Beer, and the Bottle of Cyder.

JOHN
I'll take the best care I can: but a Man would think he was got into a Fair. The Folks stare at one as if they had never seen a Man before.

[Remain **TAWDRY** and **WIFE**.

TAWDRY
Pray, Madam, is not your Ladyship infinitely tired with your Journey?

WIFE
I tired! not I, I an't tired at all; I could walk twenty Miles further.

TAWDRY
Oh, I am surprized at that; most fine Ladies are horribly fatigued after a Journey.

WIFE
Are they?—Hum! I don't know whether I an't so too; yes I am, I am, horribly fatigued. (Well, I shall never find out all that a fine Lady ought to be.)

TAWDRY
Was your Ladyship never in Town before, Madam?

WIFE
No, Madam, never before that I know of.

TAWDRY
I shall be glad to wait on you, Madam, and shew you the Town.

WIFE
I am very much obliged to you, Madam: and I am resolved to see every thing that is to be seen: The Tower, and the Crowns, and the Lions, and Bedlam, and the Parliament-House, and the Abbey—

TAWDRY
O fie, Madam! these are only Sights for the Vulgar; no fine Ladies go to these.

WIFE
No! why then I won't neither. Oh odious Tower, and filthy Lions.—But pray, Madam, are there no Sights for a fine Lady to see?

TAWDRY
O yes, Madam; there are Ridottos, Masquerades, Court, Plays, and a thousand others, so many, that a fine Lady has never time to be at home, but when she is asleep.

WIFE
I am glad to hear that; for I hate to be at home: But, dear Madam, do tell me—for I suppose you are a fine Lady.

TAWDRY
At your Service, Madam.

WIFE

What do your fine Ladies do at these Places? what do they do at Masquerades now? for I have heard of them in the Country.

TAWDRY
Why they dress themselves in a strange Dress, and they walk up and down the Room, and they cry, Do you know me? and then they burst out a laughing, and then they sit down, and then they get up, and then they walk about again, and then they go home.

WIFE
Oh, this is charming, and easy too; I shall be able to do a Masquerade in a Minute: Well, but do tell me a little of the rest. What do they do at your what d'ye call 'ems, your Plays?

TAWDRY
Why, if they can, they take a Stage-Box, where they let the Footman sit the two first Acts, to shew his Livery; then they come in to shew themselves, spread their Fans upon the Spikes, make Curt'sies to their Acquaintance, and then talk and laugh as loud as they are able.

WIFE
O delightful. By Gole, I find there is nothing in a fine Lady; any body may be a fine Lady if this be all.

AIR I
If Flaunting, and Ranting,
If Noise and Gallanting
Be all in fine Ladies requir'd;
I'll warrant I'll be
As fine a Lady
As ever in Town was admir'd.
At Plays I will rattle,
Tittle-tattle,
Tittle-tattle,
Prittle-prattle,
Prittle-prattle,
As gay and as loud as the best:
And at t'other Place,
With a Mask on my Face,
I'll ask all I see
Do you know me?
Do you know me?
And te he, he,
And te, he, he!
At nothing as loud as a Jest.

[**THOMAS** and **HAYCOCK** return.

MR. THOMAS
My Dear, I have seen the Rooms, and they are very handsome, and fit for us People of Fashion.

WIFE

Miss Lucy in Town by Henry Fielding

MISS LUCY IN TOWN. A SEQUEL TO THE VIRGIN UNMASQUED. A FARCE; WITH SONGS

Henry Fielding was born at Sharpham Park, near Glastonbury, in Somerset on April 22nd 1707. His early years were spent on his parents' farm in Dorset before being educated at Eton.

An early romance ended disastrously and with it his removal to London and the beginnings of a glittering literary career; he published his first play, at age 21, in 1728.

He was prolific, sometimes writing six plays a year, but he did like to poke fun at the authorities. His plays were thought to be the final straw for the authorities in their attempts to bring in a new law. In 1737 The Theatrical Licensing Act was passed. At a stroke political satire was almost impossible. Fielding was rendered mute. Any playwright who was viewed with suspicion by the Government now found an audience difficult to find and therefore Theatre owners now toed the Government line.

Fielding was practical with the circumstances and ironically stopped writing to once again take up his career in the practice of law and became a barrister after studying at Middle Temple. By this time he had married Charlotte Craddock, his first wife, and they would go on to have five children. Charlotte died in 1744 but was immortalised as the heroine in both Tom Jones and Amelia.

Fielding was put out by the success of Samuel Richardson's Pamela, or Virtue Rewarded. His reaction was to spur him into writing a novel. In 1741 his first novel was published; the successful Shamela, an anonymous parody of Richardson's novel.

Undoubtedly the masterpiece of Fielding's career was the novel Tom Jones, published in 1749. It is a wonderfully and carefully constructed picaresque novel following the convoluted and hilarious tale of how a foundling came into a fortune.

Fielding was a consistent anti-Jacobite and a keen supporter of the Church of England. This led to him now being richly rewarded with the position of London's Chief Magistrate. Fielding continued to write and his career both literary and professional continued to climb.

In 1749 he joined with his younger half-brother John, to help found what was the nascent forerunner to a London police force, the Bow Street Runners. Fielding's ardent commitment to the cause of justice in the 1750s unfortunately coincided with a rapid deterioration in his health. Such was his decline that in the summer of 1754 he travelled, with Mary and his daughter, to Portugal in search of a cure. Gout, asthma, dropsy and other afflictions forced him to use crutches. His health continued to fail alarmingly.

Henry Fielding died in Lisbon two months later on October 8th, 1754.

Index of Contents

MISS LUCY IN TOWN
HENRY FIELDING – A SHORT BIOGRAPHY
HENRY FIELDING – A CONCISE BIBLIOGRAPHY

DRAMATIS PERSONÆ
MEN
Goodwill
Thomas
Lord Bawble
Mr. Zorobabel
Signor Cantileno
Mr. Ballad
WOMEN
Haycock
Wife
Tawdry

SCENE: Mrs. Haycock's.

HAYCOCK and **TAWDRY**.

HAYCOCK
And he did not give you a single Shilling?

TAWDRY
No, upon my Honour.

HAYCOCK
Very well. They spend so much Money in Shew and Equipage, that they can no more pay their Ladies than their Tradesmen. If it was not for Mr. Zorobabel, and some more of his Persuasion, I must shut up my Doors.

TAWDRY
Besides, Ma'am, virtuous Women and Gentlemen's Wives come so cheap, that no Man will go to the Price of a Lady of the Town.

HAYCOCK
I thought Westminster-Hall would have given them a Surfeit of their virtuous Women: But I see nothing will do; tho' a Jury of Cuckolds were to give never such swinging Damages, it will not deter Men from qualifying more Jurymen. In short, nothing can do us any service but an Act of Parliament to put us down.

O my Dear, I am extremely glad on't. Do you know me? Ha, ha, ha, my Dear,—

[Stretching out her Fan before her.

—ha, ha, ha!

MR. THOMAS
Heyday! What's the matter now?

WIFE
I am only doing over a fine Lady at a Masquerade or Play, that's all.
[She coquets apart with her Husband.

TAWDRY [To **HAYCOCK**]
She's Simplicity itself. A Card Fortune has dealt you, which it's impossible for you to play ill. You may bring her to any Purpose.

HAYCOCK
I am glad to hear it; for she's really pretty, and I shall scarce want a Customer for a Tit-bit.

WIFE
Well, my Dear, you won't stay long, for you know I can hardly bear you out of my Sight; I shall be quite miserable till you come back, my dear, dear Tommy.

MR. THOMAS
My dear Lucy, I will but go find out a Taylor, and be back with you in an Instant.

WIFE
Pray do, my Dear.—Nay, t'other Kiss; one more,—oh! thou art the sweetest Creature.

WIFE
Well Miss, fine Lady, pray how do you like my Husband? Is he not a charming Man?

TAWDRY
Your Husband! dear Madam, and was it your Husband that you kiss'd so?

WIFE
Why, don't fine Ladies kiss their Husbands?

TAWDRY
No, never.

WIFE
O-la! but I do not like that tho'; by Gole, I believe I shall never be a fine Lady, if I must not be kiss'd. I like being a fine Lady in other Things, but not in that; I thank you. If your fine Ladies are never kiss'd, by Gole, I think we have not so much Reason to envy them as I imagin'd.

SONG

How happy are the Nymphs and Swains,
Who skip it, and trip it, all over the Plains;
How sweet are the Kisses,
How soft are the Blisses,
Transporting the Lads, and all melting their Misses? If Ladies here so nice are grown,
Who jaunt it, and flaunt it, all over the Town,
To fly as from Ruin,
From Billing and Cooing,
A Fig for their Airs, give me plain
Country Wooing.

TAWDRY

O you mistake me, Madam; a fine Lady may kiss any Man but her Husband—You will have all the Beaus in Town at your Service.

WIFE

Beaus! O Gemini, those are the Things Miss Jenny used to talk of.—And pray, Madam, do Beaus kiss so much sweeter and better than other Folks?

TAWDRY

Hum! I can't say much of that.

WIFE

And pray then, why must I like them better than my own Husband?

HAYCOCK

Because it's the Fashion, Madam. Fine Ladies do every Thing because it's the Fashion. They spoil their Shapes, to appear big with Child, because it's the Fashion. They lose their Money at Whisk, without understanding the Game; they go to Auctions, without intending to buy; they go to Operas, without any Ear; and slight their Husbands without disliking them; and all—because it is the Fashion.

WIFE

Well, I'll try to be as much in Fashion as I can: But pray when must I go to these Beaus; for I really long to see them? For Miss Jenny says, she's sure I shall like them; and if I do, i'facks! I believe I shall tell them so, notwithstanding what our Parson says.

HAYCOCK

Bravely said; I will shew you some fine Gentlemen, which I warrant you will like.

WIFE

And will they like me?

TAWDRY

Like you! they'll adore you, they'll worship you. Madam, Says my Lord, You are the most charming, beautiful, fine Creature that ever my Eyes beheld.

WIFE

What's that? Do, say that over again.

TAWDRY [Repeats]
Madam, you are, &c.

WIFE
And will they think all this of me?

TAWDRY
No doubt of it. They'll swear it.

WIFE
Then to be sure they will, think it. Yes, yes, to be sure they will think so. I wish I could see these charming Men.

HAYCOCK
O you will see them every where. Here in the House I have several to visit me, who have said the same thing to me and this young Lady.

WIFE
What did they call you charming and beautiful?—By Gole, I think they may very well say so to me [Aside] But when will these charming Men come?

HAYCOCK
They'll be here immediately: But your Ladyship will dress yourself. I see your Man has brought your Things. I suppose your Ladyship has your Clothes with you.

WIFE
Oh yes, I have Clothes enough; I have a fine Thread Satin Suit of Clothes of all the Colours in the Rainbow; then I have a fine red Gown flower'd with Yellow, all my own Work; and a fine lac'd Suit of Pinners, that was my Great Grandmother's! that has been worn but twice these forty Years, and my Mother told me, cost almost four Pounds when it was new, and reaches down hither. And then I have a great Gold Watch that hath continued in our Family, I can't tell how long, and is almost as broad as a moderate Punch Bowl; and then I have two great Gold Ear-Rings, and six or seven Rings for my Finger, worth above twenty Pound all together; and a thousand fine Things that you shall see.

HAYCOCK
Ay, Madam, these Things would have drest your Ladyship very well an hundred Years ago: But the Fashions are altered. Laced Pinners, indeed! You must cut off your Hair, and get a little Perriwig, and a French Cap; and instead of a great Watch, you must have one so small, that it is impossible it should go; and—But come, this young Lady will instruct You. Pray, Miss, wait on the Lady to her Apartment, and send for proper Tradesmen to dress her; such as the fine Ladies use. Madam, you shall be drest as you ought to be.

WIFE
Thank you, Madam; and then I shall be as fine a Lady as the best of them. By Gole, this London is a charming Place. If ever my Husband gets me out of it again, I am mistaken. Come, dear Miss, I am impatient. Do you know me? ha, he, ha!

[Exit **WIFE** and **TAWDRY**.

[Enter **LORD BAWBLE**.

So, Old Midnight, what Schemes art thou plodding on?

HAYCOCK
O fie! my Lord; I protest, if Sir Thomas and you don't leave off your Midnight Riots, you will ruin the Reputation of my House for ever. I wonder too, you have no more Regard to your own Characters.

LORD BAWBLE
Why, thou old canting Offspring of Hypocrisy, dost thou think that Men of Quality are to be confined to the Rules of Decency, like sober Citizens, as if they were ashamed of their Sins, and afraid they should lose their Turn of being Lord Mayor?

HAYCOCK
We ought all to be ashamed of our Sins. O my Lord, my Lord, had you but heard that excellent Sermon, on Kennington Common, it would have made you ashamed: I am sure it had so good an Effect upon me, that I shall be ashamed of my Sins as long as I live.

LORD BAWBLE
Why don't you leave them off then, and lay down your House?

HAYCOCK
Alas, I can't, I can't; I was bred up in the Way: But I repent heartily; I repent every Hour of my Life; and that I hope will make Amends.

LORD BAWBLE
Well, where is my Jenny Ranter?

HAYCOCK
Ah, poor Jenny! Poor Jenny is gone. I shall never see her more; she was the best of Girls; it almost breaks my tender Heart to think on't: Nay, I shall never out-live her Loss,—
[Crying]
My Lord, Sir Thomas and you forgot to pay for that Bowl of Punch last Night.

LORD BAWBLE
Damn your Punch, is my dear Jenny dead?

HAYCOCK
Worse if possible.—She is—she is turn'd Methodist, and married to one of the Brethren.

LORD BAWBLE
O, if that be all, we shall have her again.

HAYCOCK
Alas! I fear not; for they are powerful Men, and put such good Things into Women.—But pray, my Lord, how go the Finances, for I have such a Piece of Goods, such a Girl just arrived out of the Country!—upon

my Soul as pure a Virgin—for I have known her whole bringing up: She is a Relation of mine; her Father left me her Guardian. I have just brought her from a Boarding-School to have her under my own Eye, and complete her Education.

LORD BAWBLE
Where is she? let me see her.

HAYCOCK
Not a Step without the Ready. I told you I was her Guardian, and I shall not betray my Trust.

LORD BAWBLE
If I like her—upon my Honour—

HAYCOCK
I have too much value for your Lordship's Honour, to have it left in pawn. Besides, I have more Right Honourable Honour in my hands unredeemed already, than I know what to do with. However, I think you may depend on my Honour; deposite a cool Hundred, and you shall see her; and then take either the Lady or the Money.

LORD BAWBLE
I know thee to be inexorable. I'll step home and fetch the Money. I gave that Sum to my Wife this Morning to buy her Clothes. I'll take it from her again, and let her tick with the Tradesmen. Look'e, if this be stale Goods, I'll break every Window in the House.

HAYCOCK
I'll give you leave. He'll be tir'd of her in a Week, and then I may dispose of her again. I am afraid I did wrong in putting her off for a Virgin, for she'll certainly discover she is married. However, I can forswear the knowing it.

[**ZOROBABEL** brought in, in a Chair, with the Curtains drawn.

O here's one of my sober Customers.—Mr. Zorobabel, is it you? I am your Worship's most obedient Servant.

ZOROBABEL
How do you do, Mrs. Haycock? I hope no body sees or over-hears. This is an early Hour for me to visit at. I have but just been at home to dress me, since I came from the Alley.

HAYCOCK
I suppose your Worship's Hands are pretty full there now with your Lottery-Tickets?

ZOROBABEL
Fuller than I desire, Mrs. Haycock, I assure you. We hoped to have brought them to seven Pounds before this; that would have been a pretty comfortable Interest for our Money.—But, have you any worth seeing in your House?

HAYCOCK
O Mr. Zorobabel! such a Piece! such an Angel!

ZOROBABEL

Ay, ay, where? where?

HAYCOCK

Here in the House.

ZOROBABEL

Let me see her this instant.

HAYCOCK

Sure nothing was ever so unfortunate!

ZOROBABEL

Hey! what?

HAYCOCK

O Sir! not thinking to see your Worship this busy Time, I have promised her to Lord Bawble.

ZOROBABEL

How, Mrs. Haycock, promise her to a Lord without offering her to me first? Let me tell you, 'tis an Affront not only to me, but to all my Friends: And you deserve never to have any but Christians in your House again.

HAYCOCK

Marry forbid! Don't utter such Curses against me.

ZOROBABEL

Who is it supports you? Who is it can support you? Who have any Money besides us?

HAYCOCK

Pray your Worship forgive me.

ZOROBABEL

No, I will deal higher for the future, with those who are better acquainted with Lords; they will know whom to prefer. I must tell you, you are a very ungrateful Woman. I know a Woman of Fashion at St. James 's end of the Town, where I might deal cheaper than with yourself; tho' I own indeed, yours is rather the more reputable House of the two.

HAYCOCK

But my Lord hath never seen her yet.

ZOROBABEL

Hath he not? Why then he never shall, 'till I have done with her: She'll be good enough for a Lord half a year hence. Come, fetch her down, fetch her down. How long hath she been in Town?

HAYCOCK

Not two Hours. Pure Country innocent Flesh and Blood.—But what shall I say to my Lord?

ZOROBABEL
Say any thing: Put off some body else upon him; a stale Woman of Quality, or somebody who hath been in Westminster-Hall and the News-Papers.

HAYCOCK
Well, I'll do the best I can; tho', upon my Honour, I was to have had 200 Guineas from my Lord.

ZOROBABEL
Two hundred Promises you mean; but had it been ready Cash, I'll make you amends if I like her; we'll never differ about the Price; so fetch her, fetch her.

HAYCOCK
I will, an't please your Worship.

[Exit.

ZOROBABEL
Soh! the Money of Christian Men pays for the Beauty of Christian Women.—A good Exchange!

[Enter **HAYCOCK**.

[A Noise without.

HAYCOCK
O Sir, here are some noisy People coming this way; slip into the next Room: I am as tender of your Reputation as of my own.

ZOROBABEL
You are a sensible Woman, and I commend your Care; for Reputation is the very Soul of a Jew.

HAYCOCK
Go in here, I will quickly clear the Coast for you again.

[Exit **ZOROBABEL**

Now for my Gentlemen; and if I mistake not their Voices, one is an Opera-Singer, and the other a Singer in one of our Playhouses.

[Enter **SIGNIOR CANTILENO** and **MR. BALLAD**.

HAYCOCK
What is the matter, Gentlemen? what is the matter?

CANTILENO
Begar I vil ave de Woman; begar I vil ave her.

MR BALLAD

You must win her first, Signor; and if you can gain her Affections, I am too much an Englishman to think of restraining her from pursuing her own Will.

CANTILENO
Never fear, me vin her. No English Woman can withstand the Charms of my Voice.

HAYCOCK
If he begins to sing, there will be no end on't. I must go look after my young Lady.

SONG
CANTILENO
Music sure hath Charms to move,
With my Song, with my Song I'll charm my Love.
This good Land, where Money grows,
Well the Price of Singing knows:
Hither all the Warblers throng;
Taking Money,
Milk and Honey,
Taking Money for a Song.

MR BALLAD
Ha, ha, ha! What the devil should an Italian Singer do with a Mistress?

CANTILENO
Ask your Women, who are in love with the Italian Singers.

SONG
See, while I strike the vocal Lyre,
Beauty languish, languish and expire:
Like Turtle-Doves, in wooing Fit,
See the blooming Charmers sit;
Softly sighing,
Gently dying,
While sweet Sounds to Raptures move:
Trembling, thrilling,
Sweetly killing,
Airs that fan the Wings of Love.

SONG
MR BALLAD
I.
Be gone thou Shame of Human Race,
The noble Roman Soil's Disgrace;
Nor vainly with a Briton dare
Attempt to win a British Fair.

II.
For manly Charms the British Dame

Shall feel a fiercer nobler Flame;
To manly Numbers lend her Ear,
And scorn thy soft enervate Air.

[Enter a **PORTER**.

PORTER [To **CANTILENO**]
Sir, the Lady's in the next Room.

CANTILENO
Ver vel. Begar I vil ave her.

MR BALLAD
I'll follow you, and see how far the Charms of your Voice will prevail.

[Enter **ZOROBABEL**, **HAYCOCK**, and **WIFE**.

HAYCOCK [To her entering]
I am going to introduce your Ladyship to one of our fine Gentlemen whom I told you of.

WIFE [Surveying him aukwardly]
Is this a Beau, and a fine Gentleman?—By Goles Mr. Thomas is a finer Gentleman, in my Opinion, a thousand times.

ZOROBABEL
Madam, your humble Servant; I shall always think myself obliged to Mrs. Haycock for introducing me to a young Lady of your perfect Beauty. Pray, Madam, how long have you been in Town?

WIFE
Why, I have been in Town about three Hours: I am but a Stranger here, Sir; but I was very lucky to meet with this civil Gentlewoman and this fine Lady, to teach me how to dress and behave myself. Sir, I would not but be a fine Lady for all the World.

ZOROBABEL
Madam, you are in the right on't: And this soft Hand, this white Neck, and these sweet Lips were formed for no other purpose.

WIFE
Let me alone mun, will you; I won't be pull'd and hall'd about by you, I won't.—For I am very sure you don't kiss half so sweet as Mr. Thomas.

ZOROBABEL
Nay, be not coy, my Dear; if you will suffer me to kiss you, I will make you the finest of Ladies; you shall have Jewels equal to a Woman of Quality:—Nay, I will furnish a House for you in any Part of the Town, and you shall ride in a fine gilt Chair, carried by two stout Fellows, that I will keep for no other purpose.

HAYCOCK

Madam, if you will but like this Gentleman, he'll make you a fine Lady: 'Tis he, and some more of his acquaintance, that make half the fine Ladies in Town.

WIFE
Ay! Why then I will like him.—I will say I do, which I suppose is the same thing. [aside.] But when shall I have all these fine Things? for I long to begin.

ZOROBABEL
And so do I, my Angel.

[Offering to kiss her.

WIFE
—Nay, I won't kiss any more, 'till I have something in my Hand; that I am resolved of.

HAYCOCK [To **ZOROBABEL**]
Fetch her some Bawbles; any Toys will do.

WIFE
But if you will fetch me all the Things you promised me, you shall kiss me as long as you please.

ZOROBABEL
But when I have done all these things, you must never see any other Man but me.

WIFE
Must not I?—But I don't like that.—And will you stay with me always then?

ZOROBABEL
No; I shall only come to see you in the Evening.

WIFE
O then it will be well enough,—for I will see whom I please all the Day, and you shall know nothing of the matter.

[Aside.

Indeed I won't see any body else but you; indeed I won't. But do go and fetch me these fine Things.

ZOROBABEL
I go, my Dear. Mrs. Haycock, pray take care of her. I never saw any one so pretty nor so silly.

WIFE
I heard you, Sir; but you shall find I have sense enough to out-wit you. Well, Miss Jenny may stay in the Country if she will; and see nothing but the great jolly Parson, who never gives any thing but a Nosegay, or an handful of Nuts for a Kiss. But where's the young Lady that was here just now? for to my mind I am in a new World, and my Head is quite turn'd giddy.

HAYCOCK

It is a common Effect, Madam, which the Town-Air hath on young Ladies, when first they come into it.

[Enter **CANTILENO**.

CANTILENO
Begar dat dam English Ballad-singing Dog hath got away de Woman.—ah, pardie—voila une autre—

[Going towards her,

HAYCOCK
Hold, hold, Signor; this Lady is not for you.—She is a Woman of Quality, and her Price is a little beyond your Pocket.

CANTILENO
Begar I like none but de Woman of Quality.—And you no know the Price of my Pocket.—See here—begar here are fifty Guineas—dey are not above the Value of two Song.

SONG
To Beauty compar'd, pale Gold I despise;
No Jewels can sparkle like Cælia's bright Eyes:
Let Misers with pleasure survey their bright Mass;
With far greater Raptures I view my fine Lass:
Gold lock'd in my Coffers for me has no Charms;
Then its Value I own,
Then I prize it alone,
When it tempts blooming Beauty to fly to my Arms.

WIFE
This is certainly one of those Operish Singers Miss Jenny used to talk of, and to mimic: She taught me to mimic them too.

CANTILENO
Brightest Nymph turn here thy Eyes,
Behold thy Swain despairs and dies.

WIFE
A Voice so sweet cannot despair,
Unless from Deafness, of the Fair;
Such Sounds must move the dullest Ear:
Less sweet the warbling Nightingale;
Less sweet the Breeze sweeps thro' the Vale.

SONG

CANTILENO
Sweetest Cause of all my Pain,
Pride and Glory of the Plain,
See my Anguish,

See me languish:
Pity thy expiring Swain.

WIFE
Gentle Youth, of my Disdain,
Ah, too cruel you complain;
My tender Heart
Feels greater smart;
Pity me expiring Swain.

CANTILENO
Will you then all my Pangs despise?
Will Nothing your Disdain remove?

WIFE
Wife.
Can you not read my wishing Eyes?
Ah, must I tell you that I love?

CANTILENO
I faint, I die.

WIFE
Wife.
And so do I.

[**BALLAD** enters, and sings.

SONG
Turn hither your Eyes, bright Maid,
Turn hither with all your Charms;
Behold a jolly young Blade,
Who longs to be clasp'd in your Arms:
To sighing and whining,
To sobbing and pining,
Then merrily bid adieu.

CANTILENO
See how I expire.

MR BALLAD
See how I'm on fire,
And burn, my dear Nymph, for you.

WIFE
Thus strongly pursu'd,
By two Lovers woo'd,
What shall a poor Woman do?

But a Lover in Flames,
Sure most Pity claims,
So, jolly Lad, I'm for you.

[Enter **HAYCOCK**.

HAYCOCK
Gentlemen, I must beg you would go into another Room; for my Lord Bawble is just coming, and he hath bespoke this.

CANTILENO
Le Diable! one of our Directors! I would not ave him see me here for de Varld.

WIFE
Is my Lord come? How eagerly I long to see him!

CANTILENO
Allons, Madam.

WIFE
No, I will stay with my Lord.

HAYCOCK
He is just coming in.—Upon my Soul I will bring her to you presently.

CANTILENO
Well, you are de Woman of Honour.

MR BALLAD
This new Face will not come to my Turn yet; so I will to my dear Tawdry.

[Enter **LORD BAWBLE**.

LORD BAWBLE
Well, I have kept my Word; I have brought the Ready. [seeing Wife.] Upon my Soul, a fine Girl! I suppose this is she you told me of?

HAYCOCK
What shall I do? [aside.] Yes, yes, my Lord, this is the same: But pray come away; for I can't bring her to any thing yet; she is so young, if you speak to her, you will frighten her out of her Wits; have but a little Patience, and I shall bring her to my Mind.

LORD BAWBLE
Don't tell me of Patience; I'll speak to her now; and I warrant, I bring her to my Mind.

[They talk apart.

WIFE [At the other End of the Stage, looking at my **LORD BAWBLE**]

O la! That is a fine Gentleman, indeed; and yet who knows, but Mr. Thomas might be just such another, if he had but as fine Clothes on?—I wonder he don't speak to me, to be sure he don't like me; if he did, he would speak to me; and if he does not presently, the old Fellow will be back again, and then I must not talk with him.

HAYCOCK
Consider, she is just fresh and raw out of the Country.

LORD BAWBLE
I like her the better. It is in vain to contend; for, by Jupiter, I'll at her. I know how to deal with Country Ladies. I learnt the Art of making Love to them at my Election.

HAYCOCK
What will become of me! I'll get out of the way, and swear to Mr. Zorobabel, I know nothing of my Lord's seeing her.

[Exit.

LORD BAWBLE
It is generous in you, Madam, to leave the Country, to make us happy here, with the Sunshine of your Beauty.

WIFE
Sir, I am sure, I shall be very glad, if any thing in my power can make the Beaus and fine Gentlemen of this fine Town happy.—He talks just like Mr Thomas, before I was married to him, when he first came out of his Town-Service.

LORD BAWBLE
She seems delightfully ignorant. A Quality which is to me a great Recommendation of a Mistress, or a Friend.—O, Madam, can you doubt of your Power, which is as extensive as your Beauty; which lights such a Fire in the Heart of every Beholder, as nothing but your Frowns can put out.

WIFE
I'll never frown again; for if all the fine Gentlemen in Town were in love with me,—icod, with all my Heart, the more the merrier.

LORD BAWBLE
When they know you have my Admiration, you will soon have a thousand other Adorers. If a Lady hath a mind to bring Custom to her House, she hath nothing more to do but to hang one of us Lords out for a Sign.

WIFE
A Lord!—Gemini, and are you a Lord?

LORD BAWBLE
My Lord Bawble, Madam, at your Service.

WIFE

Well, my Lord Bawble is the prettiest Name I ever heard; the very Name is enough to charm one.—My Lord Bawble!

LORD BAWBLE
Why, truly, I think it hath something of a Quality Sound in it.

WIFE
Heigh, ho!

LORD BAWBLE
Why do you sigh, my Charmer?

WIFE
At what, perhaps, will make you sigh too, when you know it.

LORD BAWBLE
Ay, what?

WIFE
I am married to an odious Footman, and can never be my Lady Bawble.—I am afraid you won't like me, now I have told you.—But I assure you, if I had not been married already, I should have married you of all the Beaus and fine Gentlemen in the World: But tho' I am married to him, I like you the best; and I hope that will do.

LORD BAWBLE
Yes, yes, yes, my Dear; do!—very well: (Is this Wench an Idiot, or a Bite? marry me, with a Pox!) [Aside]
And so you are married to a Footman, my Dear?

WIFE
Yes, I am; I see you don't like me, now you know I am another Man's Wife.

LORD BAWBLE
Indeed you are mistaken; I dislike no Man's Wife but my own.

WIFE
O-la: What are you married then?

LORD BAWBLE
Yes, I think I am: But I have almost forgot it; for I have not seen my Wife, 'till this Morning, for a Twelvemonth.

WIFE
No! by Goles, you may marry somebody else for me. And now I think on't; if I should be seen speaking to him, I shall lose all the fine things I was promised.

LORD BAWBLE
What are you considering, my Dear?

WIFE

I must not stay with you any longer, for I expect an old Gentleman every Minute, who promised me a thousand fine Things, if I would not speak to any body but him: He promised to keep two tall lusty Fellows for no other Business but to carry me up and down in a Chair.

LORD BAWBLE

I will not only do that, but I will keep you two other tall Fellows for no other Use but to walk before your Chair.

WIFE

Will you? Nay, I assure you, I like you better than him, if I shall not lose any fine Things by the bargain.— But hold, now I think on't: Suppose I stay here till he come back again with his Presents, I can take the Things, promise him, and go with you afterwards, you know, my Lord. Oh, how pretty Lord sounds!

LORD BAWBLE

No, you will have no need on't; I will give you Variety of fine things. ('Till I am tired of you, and then I'll take them away again.) But, my Dear, these Lodgings are not fine enough; I will take some finer for you.

WIFE

O la! what are there finer Houses than this in Town? Why, my Father hath five Hundred a Year in the Country, and his House is not half so fine.

LORD BAWBLE

O, my Dear, Gentlemen of no hundred Pounds a Year scorn such an House as this: No body lives now in any thing but a Palace.

WIFE

Nay, the finer the better, by Goles, if you will pay for it.

LORD BAWBLE

Pugh, p'shaw, pay! never mind that: That Word hath almost put me in the Vapours.—Come, my dear Girl—

[Kisses her.

WIFE

O fie, my Lord, you make me blush. He kisses sweeter than my Husband, a thousand times; I did not think there had been such a Man as my Husband in the World, but I find I was mistaken.

LORD BAWBLE

Consider, my Dear, what a Pride you will have in hearing the Man you love call'd, Lordship.

WIFE

Lordship! it is pretty. Lordship!—But then you won't see me above once in a Twelvemonth.

LORD BAWBLE

I will see you every Day, every Minute: I like you so well, that nothing but being married to you could make me hate you.

WIFE
O Gemini! I forgot it was the Fashion.

LORD BAWBLE
Let us lose no time, but hasten to find some Place where I may equip you like a Woman of Quality.

WIFE
I am out of my Wits. My Lord, I am ready to wait on Lordship, wherever Lordship pleases.—Lordship! Quality! I shall be a fine Lady immediately now.

[Enter **HAYCOCK**.

HAYCOCK
What shall I do? I am ruin'd for ever! My Lord hath carried away the Girl. Mr. Zorobabel will never forgive me; I shall lose him and all his Friends, and they are the only Support of my House. Foolish Slut, to prefer a rakish Lord to a sober Jew: But Women never know how to make their Market 'till they are so old, no one will give any thing for them.

[Enter **THOMAS**.

MR. THOMAS
Your humble Servant, Madam. Pray, Madam, how do you like my Clothes?

HAYCOCK
Your Taylor hath been very expeditious, indeed, Sir.

MR. THOMAS
Yes, Madam, I should not have had them so soon, but that I met with an old Acquaintance, Tom Shabby, the Taylor in Monmouth-Street, who fitted me with a Suit in a moment.—But where's my Wife?

HAYCOCK
What shall I say to him? I believe she is gone out to see the Town.

MR. THOMAS
Gone out! hey! what, without me! Who's gone with her?

HAYCOCK
Really, Sir, I can't tell. Here was a Gentleman all over Lace: I suppose, some Acquaintance of hers. I fancy she went with him.

MR. THOMAS
A Gentleman in Lace! I am undone, ruin'd, dishonour'd! Some Rascal hath betray'd away my Wife.— Zounds, why did you let her go out of the House 'till my Return?

HAYCOCK

The Lady was only a Lodger with me. I had no Power over her.

MR. THOMAS
How did any Man come to see her? for I am sure she did not know one Man in Town. It must be somebody that used to come here.

HAYCOCK
May the Devil fetch me, if ever I saw him before; nor do I know how he got in.—But there are Birds of Prey lurking in every Corner of this wicked Town: It makes me shed Tears to think what Villains there are in the World, to betray poor innocent young Ladies.

[Cries.

MR. THOMAS
Oons and the Devil! the first six Weeks of our Marriage!

HAYCOCK
That is a pity indeed,—if you have been marry'd no longer: Had you been together half a Year, it had been some Comfort. But be advised, have a little patience; in all probability whoever the Gentleman is, he'll return her again soon.

MR. THOMAS
Return her! ha! stain'd, spotted, sullied! Who shall return me my Honour?—S'Death! I'll search her thro' the Town, the World.—Ha! my Father here!

GOODWILL [Entering]
Son, I met your Man John at the Inn, and he shew'd me the way hither.—Where is my Daughter, your Wife?

MR. THOMAS
Stolen! lost! every thing is lost, and I am undone.

GOODWILL
Hey-day! What's the matter?

MR. THOMAS
The matter! O curse this vile Town; I did but go to furnish myself with a Suit of Clothes, that I might appear like a Gentleman, and in the mean time your Daughter hath taken care that I shall appear like a Gentleman all the Days of my Life; for I am sure I shall be ashamed to shew my Head among Footmen.

GOODWILL
How! My Daughter run away?—

HAYCOCK
I am afraid it is too true.

GOODWILL
And do you stand meditating?

MR. THOMAS
What shall I do?

GOODWILL
Go advertise her this Minute in the News-Paper;—get my Lord Chief Justice's Warrant.

HAYCOCK
As for the latter, it may be advisable; but the former will be only throwing away your Money; for the Papers have been of late so crammed with Advertisements of Wives running from their Husbands, that no body now reads them.

MR. THOMAS
That I should be such a Blockhead to bring my Wife to Town!

GOODWILL
That I should be such a Sot as to suffer you!

MR. THOMAS
If I was unmarried again, I would not venture my Honour in a Woman's keeping, for all the Fortune she could bring me.

GOODWILL
And if I was a young Fellow again, I would not get a Daughter, for all the Pleasure any Woman could give me.

[Enter **ZORABABEL**.

ZOROBABEL
Here, where's my Mistress? I have equipp'd her; here are Trinkets enough to supply an Alderman's Wife.

HAYCOCK
I must be discover'd. Hush, hush, consider your Reputation; here are Company.—Your Mistress is run away with my Lord Bawble .

ZOROBABEL
My Mistress run away! Damn my Reputation: Where's the Girl? I will have the Girl.

GOODWILL
This Gentleman may have lost a Daughter too.

MR. THOMAS
Or a Wife, perhaps—You have lost your Wife, Sir, by the Violence of your Rage?

ZOROBABEL
O worse, worse, Sir; I have lost a Mistress. While I went to buy her Trinkets, this damn'd Jade of a Bawd (where is she?) lets in a young Rake, and he is run away with her: The sweetest bit of Country Innocence, just come to Town. S'Blood, I would have given an hundred Lottery-Tickets for her.

GOODWILL
How, Hell-hound!

MR. THOMAS
How, Hell-hound!

HAYCOCK
I am an innocent Woman, and shall fall a Sacrifice to an unjust Suspicion.

GOODWILL
Oh! my poor Daughter!

MR. THOMAS
My Wife, that I had so much delight in!

ZOROBABEL
My Mistress, that I propos'd such Pleasure in.

HAYCOCK
O the Credit of my House, gone for ever!

ZOROBABEL
Ha! here she is again.—

[Enter WIFE.

WIFE
Such Joy! such Rapture! Well, I'll never go into the Country again. Faugh! how I hate the Name.—Oh! Father, I am sure you don't know me; nor you, Mr. Thomas, neither;—nor I won't know you.—Ah, you old fusty Fellow,—I don't want any thing you can give; nor you shan't come near me,—so you shan't.— Madam, I am very much oblig'd to you, for letting me see the World. I hate to talk to any one I can't call Lordship.

GOODWILL
And is this be-powder'd, be-curl'd, be-hoop'd Madwoman my Daughter?—

[She coquets affectedly.

Why, Hussy, don't you know your own Father?

MR. THOMAS
Nor your Husband?

WIFE
No, I don't know you at all;—I never saw you before. I have got a Lord, and I don't know any one but my Lord.

MR. THOMAS

And pray what hath my Lord done to you, that hath put you in such Raptures?

WIFE

O, by Gole! who'd be fool then? When I liv'd in the Country, I used to tell you every thing I did; but I am grown wiser now, for I am told I must never let my Husband know any thing I do, for he'd be angry; tho' I don't much care for your Anger, for I design always to live with my Lord now; and he's never to be angry, do what I will—Why, prithee, Fellow, do'st thou think that I am not fine Lady enough to know the Difference between a Lord and a Footman?

ZOROBABEL

A Footman!

HAYCOCK

I thought he was a Servant, by his talking so much of his Honour.

MR. THOMAS

You call me Footman! I own I was a Footman, and had rather be a Footman still, than a tame Cuckold to a Lord. I wish every Man, who is not a Footman, thought in the same manner.

GOODWILL

Thou art a pretty Fellow, and worthy a better Wife.

MR. THOMAS

Sir, I am sorry that from henceforth I cannot, without being a Rascal, look on your Daughter as my Wife; I am sorry I can't forgive her.

WIFE

Forgive me,—ha, ha, ha; ha, ha, ha! comical! why I won't forgive you, mun.

WIFE

What hath he done, which you will not forgive?

WIFE

Done! why I have found out somebody I like better; and he's my Husband, and I hate him, because it is the Fashion: That he hath done.

ZOROBABEL

Sir Skip, a word with you: If you intend to part with your Wife, I will give you as much for her as any Man.

MR. THOMAS

Sir!

ZOROBABEL

Sir, I say, I will give you as much, or more for your Wife, than any Man.

MR. THOMAS

Those Words, which suppose me a Villain, call me so, and thus should be return'd.

[Gives him a Box on the Ear.

ZOROBABEL
S'Death, Sir! do you know whom you use in this manner?

MR. THOMAS
Know you, yes, you Rascal, and you ought to know me. I have indeed the greatest reason to remember you, having purchas'd a Ticket of you in the last Lottery for as much again as it was worth.—However, you shall have reason to remember me for the future; a Footman shall teach such a low, pitiful, stock-jobbing Pickpocket to dare to think to cuckold his Betters.

[Kicks him off the Stage.

ZOROBABEL
You shall hear of me in Westminster-Hall.

GOODWILL
Your humble Servant.

[Kicking him off.

ZOROBABEL
Very fine! very fine!—a Ten-Thousand-Pound Man is to be kick'd!

GOODWILL
A Rascal, a Villain.

[Enter LORD BAWBLE.

WIFE
O my dear Lord, are you come?

LORD BAWBLE
Fie, my Dear, you should not have run away from me while I was in an inner Room, promising the Tradesman to pay him for your fine Things.

WIFE
O my Lord, I only stept into a Chair, as you call it, to make a Visit to a fine Lady here. It is pure Sport to ride in a Chair.

LORD BAWBLE
Bless me! what's here? My old Man Tom in masquerade?

MR. THOMAS
I give your Lordship Joy of this fine Girl—

LORD BAWBLE

Stay 'till I have had her, Tom. Egad she hath cost me a round Sum, and I have had nothing but Kisses for my Money yet.

MR. THOMAS

No, my Lord! Then I am afraid your Lordship never will have any thing more, for this Lady is mine.

LORD BAWBLE

How! what Property have you in her?

MR. THOMAS

The Property of an English Husband, my Lord.

LORD BAWBLE

How, Madam! are you married to this Man?

WIFE

I married to him! I never saw the Fellow before.

LORD BAWBLE

Tom, thou art a very impudent Fellow.

GOODWILL

Mercy on me! what a Sink of Iniquity is this Town? She hath been here but five Hours, and learnt Assurance already to deny her Husband.

LORD BAWBLE

Come, Tom, resign the Girl by fair Means, or worse will follow.

MR. THOMAS

How, my Lord, resign my Wife! Fortune, which made me poor, made me a Servant; but Nature, which made me an Englishman, preserv'd me from being a Slave. I have as good a Right to the Little I claim, as the proudest Peer hath to his great Possessions; and whilst I am able, I will defend it.

LORD BAWBLE

Ha! Rascal!

[They draw.

GOODWILL

Hold, my Lord; this Girl, ungracious as she is, is my Daughter, and this honest Man's Wife.

WIFE

Whether I am his Wife or no, is nothing to the purpose; for I will go with my Lord. I hate my Husband, and I love my Lord. He's a fine Gentleman, and I am a fine Lady, and we are fit for one another.—Now, my Lord, here are all the fine Things you gave me; he will take them away, but you will keep them for me.

LORD BAWBLE
So, now I think every Man hath his own again; and since she is your Wife, Tom, much good may do you with her. I question not but these Trinkets will purchase a finer Lady.

[Exit.

WIFE
What, is my Lord gone?

MR. THOMAS
Yes, Madam, and you shall go, as soon as I can get Horses put into a Coach.

WIFE
Ay, but I won't go with you.

MR. THOMAS
No, but you shall go without me: Your good Father here will take care of you into the Country; where, if I hear of your Amendment, perhaps, half a year hence I may visit you; for since my Honour is not wrong'd, I can forgive your Folly.

WIFE
I shall shew you, Sir, that I am a Woman of Spirit, and not to be govern'd by my Husband.—I shall have Vapours and Fits, (these they say are infallible) and if these won't do, let me see who dares carry me into the Country against my Will: I will swear the Peace against them.

GOODWILL
Oh! oh! that ever I should beget a Daughter!

MR. THOMAS
Here, John!

[JOHN [Enters]
An't please your Worship.

MR. THOMAS
Let all my Things be pack'd up again in the Coach they came in;—and send Betty here this Instant with your Mistress's Riding-Dress.—Come, Madam, you must strip yourself of your Puppet-Shew Dress, as I will of mine; they will make you ridiculous in the Country, where there is still something of Old England remaining. Come, no Words, no delay; by Heavens! if you but affect to loiter, I will send Orders with you to lock you up, and allow you only the bare Necessaries of Life. You shall know I'm your Husband, and will be obey'd.

WIFE [Crying]
And must I go into the Country by myself? Shall I not have a Husband, or a Lord, or any body?—If I must go, won't you go with me?

MR. THOMAS
Can you expect it? Can you ask me, after what hath happened?

WIFE
What I did, was only to be a fine Lady, and what they told me other fine Ladies do, and I should never have thought of in the Country; but if you will forgive me, I will never attempt to be more than a plain Gentlewoman again.

MR. THOMAS
Well, and as a plain Gentlewoman you shall have Pleasures some fine Ladies may envy. Come, dry your Eyes; my own Folly, not yours, is to blame; and that I am only angry with.

WIFE
And will you go with me then, Tommy?

MR. THOMAS
Ay, my Dear, and stay with thee too: I desire no more to be in this Town, than to have thee here.

GOODWILL
Henceforth, I will know no Degree, no Difference between Men, but what the Standards of Honour and Virtue create: The noblest Birth without these is but splendid Infamy; and a Footman with these Qualities, is a Man of Honour.

SONG
WIFE
Welcome again, ye rural Plains;
Innocent Nymphs, and virtuous Swains:
Farewell Town, and all its Sights;
Beaus and Lords, and gay Delights:
All is idle Pomp and Noise;
Virtuous Love gives greater Joys.

CHORUS
All is idle Pomp and Noise;
Virtuous Love gives greater Joys.

Henry Fielding – A Short Biography

Henry Fielding was born at Sharpham Park, near Glastonbury, in Somerset on April 22nd 1707. His early years were spent on his parents' farm in Dorset. His family were well to do. His father was a colonel, later a general in the army, his maternal grandfather was a judge of the Queen's Bench and his second cousin would later become the fourth Earl of Denbigh.

He was educated at Eton where he became lifelong friends with William Pitt the Elder.

An early romance ended disastrously and with it his removal to London and the beginnings of a glittering literary career. Early advice on this came from another cousin, the noted poet, Lady Mary Wortley Montagu. Fielding published his first play, at age 21, in 1728.

Later that same year he journeyed to the University at Leiden, the oldest University in Holland, to study classics and law. However, within months, with funds low, mainly due to his father cutting off his allowance, he was forced to return to London and to write for the theatre.

It was a twist of fate that was to ensure him both notoriety and a reputation that would exceed his wildest expectations.

He was prolific, sometimes writing six plays a year, but he did like to poke fun at the authorities. His plays were thought to be the final straw for the authorities in their attempts to bring some sense of order to an increasingly provocative Theatre. Some of the plays denigrated, insulted, or criticised either the King, or his Government, in ways that caused them to react with their preferred response; a new law. Although the Golden Rump was cited as the play on which the authorities based their need for better regulation it is thought that the constant stepping over the line by Fielding in his own works was the actual trigger for, and target of, the new law. No copy of the play, The Golden Rump, exists today and it seems never, in fact, to have been performed or perhaps even published. Various accounts attribute Fielding as the author and others say it was secretly commissioned by Walpole himself to bring about the conditions necessary to bring the Act before Parliament.

Whatever the validity in 1737 The Theatrical Licensing Act was passed. At a stroke political satire was almost impossible. Fielding much admired – and reviled – for his savaging of Sir Robert Walpole government was rendered mute. Any playwright who was viewed with suspicion by the Government now found an audience difficult to find and therefore Theatre owners now toed the Government line, works only being available for performance after review by the Lord Chamberlain. A process that was to last in England, although greatly amended in 1843, until 1968.

Fielding was practical in the circumstances and ironically stopped writing to once again take up his career in the practice of law. He became a barrister after studying at Middle Temple – he completed the six year course in only three. By this time he had also married Charlotte Craddock, his first wife, and they would go on to have five children, but only a daughter would survive. Charlotte died in 1744 but was immortalised as the heroine in both Tom Jones and Amelia.

As a businessman Fielding lacked any financial education and he and his family often endured bouts of poverty. He did however find a wealthy benefactor in the shape of Ralph Allen, who was to later feature in the novel Tom Jones as the character foundation for Squire Allworthy.

Fielding never stopped writing political satire or satires of current arts and letters. The Tragedy of Tragedies, for which Hogarth designed the frontispiece, had, for example, some success as a printed play. He also contributed a number of works to journals of the day as well as writing for Tory periodicals, usually under the name of "Captain Hercules Vinegar". His choice of name reveals his style. But then again his other later nom de plumes are also revealing; Sir Alexander Drawcansir and Scriblerus Secundus

In 1731 Fielding wrote "The Roast Beef of Old England", which is used by the Royal Navy and the United States Marine Corps. It was later arranged by Richard Leveridge.

During the late 1730s and early 1740s Fielding continued to air his liberal and anti-Jacobite views in satirical articles and newspapers. He was nothing if not passionate and this adherence to principles would eventually have great reward for him.

Fielding was much put out by the success of Samuel Richardson's Pamela, or Virtue Rewarded. His reaction was to spur him into writing a novel. In 1741 this first novel, Shamela, was a success, an anonymous parody of Richardson's melodramatic novel. It is a satire that follows the model of the famous Tory satirists of the previous generation; Swift and Gay.

On the tail of this success came Joseph Andrews in 1742. Begun as a parody on Pamela's brother, Joseph, it swiftly developed and matured into an accomplished novel in its own right and marked the entrance of Fielding as a major English novelist.

In 1743, he published a novel in the Miscellanies volume III (which was, in fact, the first volume of the Miscellanies). This was The History of the Life of the Late Mr Jonathan Wild the Great. Sometimes this is cited as his first novel, as he did indeed begin writing it before Shamela, but it is now placed later. Once again Fielding returns to satire and one of his favourite subjects – Sir Robert Walpole. In it he draws a parallel between Walpole and Jonathan Wild, the infamous gang leader and highwayman. He implicitly compares the Whig party in Parliament to a gang of thieves, whose leader, Walpole, lives only for his desire and ambition to be a "Great Man" (a common epithet for Walpole) and should culminate only in the antithesis of greatness: being hung from a gallows. By now Walpole had resigned as Prime minster after some 20 years. Fielding could now re-affirm political allegiance back to the Whigs and would now denounce both Tories and Jacobites in his writings.

Although Fielding was never afraid to court controversy he published his next work anonymously in 1746, and perhaps with good reason. The Female Husband, a fictionalized account of a sensational case of a female transvestite who was tried for duping another woman into marriage. This was one of a number of small published pamphlets at sixpence a time. Though a minor item in both length and his canon it shows Fielding's consistent interest and examination of fraud, sham, and masks but, of course, his subject matter was rather sensational.

In 1747, three years after Charlotte's death and ignoring public opinion, he married her former maid, Mary Daniel, who was pregnant. Mary bore him five children altogether; three daughters, who died early and sons William and Allen.

Undoubtedly the masterpiece of Fielding's career was the novel Tom Jones, published in 1749. It is a wonderfully and carefully constructed picaresque novel following the convoluted and hilarious tale of how a foundling came into a fortune.

Fielding was a consistent anti-Jacobite and a keen supporter of the Church of England. This led to him now being richly rewarded with the position of London's Chief Magistrate. The position itself had no salary attached but he refused all manner of bribes during his tenure, which was most unusual. Fielding continued to write and his career both literary and professional continued to climb.

In 1749 he joined with his younger half-brother John, to help found what was the nascent forerunner to a London police force, the Bow Street Runners. (He and his siblings were quite some partnership. His younger sister, Sarah, also became a well known novelist)

His influence here was undoubted. He and John did much to help the cause of judicial reform and to help improve prison conditions. His pamphlets and enquiries included a proposal for the abolition of public hangings. This was not, as you would think because he was opposed to capital punishment as such—indeed, for example, in his 1751 presiding over the trial of the notorious criminal James Field, he found him guilty in a robbery and sentenced him to hang.

In January 1752 Fielding started a fortnightly periodical titled The Covent-Garden Journal, which he would publish under the colourful pseudonym of "Sir Alexander Drawcansir, Knt. Censor of Great Britain" until November of the same year. In this periodical, Fielding directly challenged the "armies of Grub Street" and the other periodical writers of the day in a conflict that would eventually become the Paper War of 1752–3.

Fielding then published, in 1753, "Examples of the interposition of Providence in the Detection and Punishment of Murder, a work in which, rejecting the deistic and materialistic visions of the world, he wrote in favour of the belief in God's presence and divine judgement, arguing that the rise of murder rates was due to neglect of the Christian religion. In 1753 he would add to this with Proposals for making an effectual Provision for the Poor.

Fielding's ardent commitment to the cause of justice as a great humanitarian in the 1750s unfortunately coincided with a rapid deterioration in his health. Such was his decline that in the summer of 1754 he travelled, with Mary and his daughter, to Portugal in search of a cure. Gout, asthma, dropsy and other afflictions forced him to use crutches. His health continued to fail alarmingly.

Henry Fielding died in Lisbon two months later on October 8th, 1754.

His tomb is in the city's English Cemetery (Cemitério Inglês), which is now the graveyard of St. George's Church, Lisbon.

Henry Fielding – A Concise Bibliography

The Masquerade, a poem
Love in Several Masques, a play, 1728
Rape Upon Rape, a play, 1730.
The Temple Beau, a play, 1730
The Author's Farce, a play, 1730
The Letter Writers, a play, 1731
The Tragedy of Tragedies; or, The Life and Death of Tom Thumb the Great, a play, 1731
Grub-Street Opera, a play, 1731
The Roast Beef of Old England, 1731
The Modern Husband, a play, 1732
The Mock Doctor, a play, 1732
The Lottery, a play, 1732
The Covent Garden Tragedy, a play, 1732
The Miser, a play, 1732
The Old Debauchees, a play 1732
The Intriguing Chambermaid, a play, 1734

Don Quixote in England, a play, 1734

Pasquin, a play, 1736

Eurydice Hiss'd, a play, 1737

The Historical Register for the Year 1736, a play, 1737

An Apology for the Life of Mrs. Shamela Andrews, a novel, 1741

The History of the Adventures of Joseph Andrews & his Friend, Mr. Abraham Abrams, a novel, 1742

The Life and Death of Jonathan Wild, the Great, a novel, 1743.

Miscellanies – collection of works, 1743, contained the poem Part of Juvenal's Sixth Satire, Modernized in Burlesque Verse

The Female Husband or the Surprising History of Mrs Mary alias Mr George Hamilton, who was convicted of having married a young woman of Wells and lived with her as her husband, taken from her own mouth since her confinement, a pamphlet, fictionalized report, 1746

The History of Tom Jones, a Foundling, a novel, 1749

A Journey from this World to the Next – 1749

Amelia, a novel, 1751

"Examples of the interposition of Providence in the Detection and Punishment of Murder containing above thirty cases in which this dreadful crime has been brought to light in the most extraordinary and miraculous manner; collected from various authors, ancient and modern", 1752

The Covent Garden Journal, a periodical, 1752

Journal of a Voyage to Lisbon, a travel narrative, 1755

The Fathers: Or, the Good-Natur'd Man, a play, published posthumously in 1778

Other Works (Undated)

An Old Man or The Virgin Unmasked

Miss Lucy in Town, a Play, a sequel to The Virgin Unmasked

Plutus with William Young from the Greek play by Aristophanes.

The Temple Beau, a play

The Wedding Beau, a play

The Welsh Opera

Tumble-Down Dick

An Essay on Conversation, an Essay

The True Patriot, a letter

www.ingramcontent.com/pod-product-compliance
Lightning Source LLC
Chambersburg PA
CBHW021948040426
42448CB00008B/1293